foreword

John Noltner takes us on a unique journey filled with revelations of courage and commitment, resilience and hope. It is a beautiful journey that speaks to our innermost being. It touches us in a way that allows us to see the world from a different perspective. As we read about the diverse experiences of people from many different parts of our world, we begin to identify with them. Their experience, in a microcosmic way, is also our experience. But too often we are not conscious of it.

Reading this book places us, for fleeting moments, in the position of those people who are horrified by the atrocities of war, and the many who are concerned about the plight of the poor and the deprived of our world. In fact, many people are ready to assist in changing things.

We begin to learn the deep pain and humiliation suffered by people who have been oppressed in various ways. We see how their spirit remains intact through all the trials and sorrows they endure. We see their generosity and forgiveness.

The lessons we learn from these experiences are indeed important for humankind today. Important, because they are proclaiming to us, loudly and clearly, that enough is enough. We must not repeat the mistakes of the past ever again. Let us begin to heed this message.

In my own life, I have found that peace does not only mean protesting and resisting injustice, but also living our everyday lives doing big and small things to bring greater harmony to the world. Helping sick and injured children, protecting the voiceless animals, preserving the plants and trees that are being eliminated by development, and contributing in little ways to save the world by conserving, reusing, recycling, and reducing both what we need and what we discard, in the hope that the already distended Mother Earth will absorb it.

We need to appreciate the richness of our diverse heritage and begin to see the value of global citizenship, so that peace and social and political justice may prevail in the world. Perhaps it will inspire us to become peacemakers.

ELA GANDHI

artist's statement

This project is the result of almost two years of work, exploring the meaning of peace.

The seed for this book germinated as two events coincided in my journey as a photographer. The first was a restlessness I had been feeling for some time with regard to my professional work. The second event was the economic downturn, which provided me with some much-needed time for reflection and evaluation.

I was born to a social worker and an educator, so I suppose there was always fertile soil for this sort of subject matter to thrive. I have always had an interest in social justice issues, and have served on several boards for nonprofits that did good work both here and abroad.

Yet I am not an expert on peace. I have no formal training in the subject, and I hold no related academic degree. My friends and my family will tell you that I regularly miss the mark when it comes to living in harmony with others.

But celebrating perfection is not the goal for this project. It is about moving forward, about finding ways that we can bridge some of our differences, and about celebrating the common humanity that binds us.

I believe in the power of stories. I have spent my career telling stories through both images and words, and that is what I set out to do with this series.

Each of these subjects has a unique story to tell — a unique perspective on peace — and I am grateful they were willing to share it.

The premise is simple. I asked each person what peace means to him or her. In response, they have spoken about spiritual peace, political peace, and inner peace. They have shared with us how they work toward that peace in their lives and what obstacles they have encountered along the way.

a peace of my mind

may we all find peace...

☮ [signature]

dedicated to all those who long for peace in the world . . .

and to those who work toward it every day.

contents

Our world has become polarized. We quickly assess others and place them in a category. We promptly dismiss someone's viewpoint if we hear the buzzwords that tell us they are from another camp. Politically, ethnically, religiously, we expend an enormous amount of energy looking at the things that divide us. I believe we would do well to spend some time and energy looking for the things that unite us.

When we hear someone's story, he or she becomes more human to us. It is the first step in building understanding and it begins with dialogue.

None of us has all of the answers. These subjects don't. I certainly don't. But collectively, these portraits and stories weave a rich human fabric and offer us a framework to explore some possible answers together.

I encourage you to view this book as a first step. The quotes that accompany the portraits are a small portion of the subjects' interviews. These interviews exist on the project website as podcasts. Take time to listen to them and understand the context in which they made their statements. Use the interviews as stepping stones to your own conversations.

I don't doubt that we will continue to bump into each other as our human history unfolds. Conflicts will continue to arise between nations, on our streets, and in our homes. But we can take steps to move in a different direction — away from conflict and toward peace. Only by making peace a part of our regular dialogue can we hope to make progress.

We face enormous challenges as we work together to create a more peaceful world. The answers will be found by joining together in conversation.

JOHN NOLTNER

WWW.APEACEOFMYMIND.NET

David A. DeLampert Jr.

I feel it's the richest thing you got going for you is your name. As we fight in this world to obtain something for ourselves and to be somebody — nobody wants to feel like they're nobody, no matter who it is. I encourage people to believe, in my travels, that we are somebody. That everybody is somebody, regardless if you are an addict, alcoholic, or whatever. Whatever your vice is in life, I happen to believe you can be at peace with yourself. Get to know who you are. This has given me an opportunity to know me.

People are so hard on each other, nitpicking and always looking for something wrong and wanting to put someone down. People don't know how to forgive. That's the one thing the world ain't caught onto yet, forgiveness. We have a problem with forgiving each other so we gonna have a problem with being at peace with each other.

And then you got those who like to keep up a lot of razzamatazz. They like to keep up a lot of bullshit. There are those in this world who are not satisfied unless they are jamming somebody else's life up.

And to find out there are people in high places who do things like that, it kind of frustrates me, because I work hard at maintaining my own peace down here. I don't get up there. I get to stay down here. And there's a great gulf between the ones at the top and we who are at the bottom. But one more day above ground is better than one underneath, so I try to be at peace most of the time.

8

David A. De Lampert Jr. has been living on the streets of Minneapolis for the past 30 years. A veteran, he survives on disability checks and through gratuities people offer him.

David spends his days inviting people to sign his coat with a permanent marker. When they sign, they will often give him a dollar or two "to help keep me going." He has filled up more than 100 coats with signatures over the past decade, as well as hats, umbrellas, and canes.

For David, collecting signatures began as a way to survive, but eventually became a way for him to reach out to other people.

PHOTOGRAPHED 5/28/2009

Kimberley Lueck

O ne doesn't sit down on a cushion and suddenly attain peace. One sits down on a cushion and encounters the speedy nature of mind and the confused glut of thoughts and reactions. But if I sit down, if I just take that step, I'm practicing peace. Just having the courage to interrupt the status quo. And then if I go further and actually try to accommodate what arises . . . in my case, the practice would be to bring the attention to the breath. So if my attention wanders and I start thinking of somebody I'm really mad at or sick of . . . practicing peace is noticing that with some gentleness and then gently leading myself back to a breath. So there's a process of reapplying ourselves, reapplying ourselves to peace.

And then I can remember, well yes, it has to be done over and over again, until we've practiced. Like practicing scales at the piano. First your fingers bumble over it for a long time and eventually when you practice and practice, it becomes fluid and beautiful. We're not on human lifespan time. It's a big and ancient universe, and one aspect of peace is patience. Patience with ourselves and others. Patience with our impatience, even.

Kimberley Lueck is a Shambhala Buddhist minister. She is active in interfaith dialogue and helps organize an annual interfaith harvest celebration.

Kimberley finds conflict arising out of the desire to control things. If we can recognize that tendency in ourselves, there is a greater chance that we will recognize it in others and diffuse some of the tensions that arise. And if we are able to develop compassion for ourselves, there is a greater chance that we can offer it to others as well.

This is something that we can do for ourselves and for the world. When we're willing to approach our scary places, then we know that we're not alone. Everyone has scary places and if we can actually rest in that for even a few moments, we've already created some peace in the world. We've already opened the doors to realizing that we aren't separate. Maybe that's it . . . the fruitional state of peace is when we all recognize our interconnectedness.

PHOTOGRAPHED 6/2/2009

II

Hans Early-Nelson

As civilization has progressed, we've become detached from the earth and from our true primal instinct to survive and provide for ourselves. I know there was conflict and war thousands of years ago, so you can't say that it's technology or cell phones and missiles that have created unrest and disagreements around the world. But the fact that we're not providing for ourselves is a barrier. We're not connected to our purpose to survive. We're so well provided for that we kind of don't know what to do in the world. I feel that way sometimes.

We're also so confined in this space. We're bumping up on each other all the time. I think a lot of it has to do with people needing to be places and feeling like there's never enough time. And that translates to "you're in my way."

I believe in survival of the fittest, in many ways, and so there's always going to be some kind of conflict. I prefer there to not be war and bloodshed, but I feel like conflict is our inherent way of working our differences out. The ideal peaceful world to me would be rid of violence, but there'd still be altercations. There'd still be some wrestling and some jaunting and I feel like we can achieve that. Perhaps get rid of the warheads and all the guns. I prefer there not to be enraged violence to the point of killing people or maiming people, but there would be scuffles, there would be bruises.

Hans Early-Nelson is a metal sculptor and artist. An avid biker and swimmer, he talks about learning to live in a community.

Hans sees himself as a mediator and offers as an example of urban justice a time when he witnessed a robbery. He tracked down the thief and convinced him to return the money to its rightful owner. In the process, Hans learned something about the thief's history and wound up giving him $10 of his own money as a reward for returning the cash he had just stolen.

12

PHOTOGRAPHED 5/21/2009

Fred and Judy Baron

Judy: It wasn't a community. It was a bunch of people who were afraid to be dead the next minute. There could be no peace in a place like that.

Fred: I have hope that we learn from each other, that each generation learns from the previous one. I do realize that the learning process is difficult and has its ups and downs. But we have learned so much, we have achieved so much in our relatively short human existence. We can send a man to the moon and bring him back. We are routinely sending objects around the globe. We have stations in outer space. We can build atomic bombs and atomic research centers and atomic installations for good and for bad. We can take the organs out from one person and place them into another to give them life. We have done unimaginable things. We have created tiny little objects and apertures that can talk to us. They can do things mathematically and scientifically that took people a generation and they can do this in a matter of seconds. So we have reduced time and space and effort and whatnot. But in the way we relate to each other in a personal way — person to person and people to people — progress is much more difficult and much slower. That is what we have to strive for.

Fred and Judy Baron are survivors of Nazi death camps. They met after they were liberated from the camps and were recovering in a hospital in Sweden. They moved to America, got married, and started a family.

They recall the absolute absence of peace in the camps and how they found peace again in their lives. Both Fred and Judy feel strongly that it is our obligation to look after one another in this world, especially those who are less fortunate than ourselves.

14

PHOTOGRAPHED 6/14/2010

Odeh Muhawesh

We — the followers of Islam and the followers of Christianity — have to say to the world, to these [extremists], don't speak on my behalf. Don't start a war on my behalf. Don't bomb the World Trade Center on my behalf. Don't start a war in another country in the name of my faith.

In many of my speeches, I always tell people this: Imagine if Moses, Jesus, and Mohammad came today and stood in front of us. Moses would ask his followers, "What have you done?" And Jesus would ask his followers, "What have you done?" And Mohammad would ask his followers, "What have you done?"

They all would be ashamed of us. They all would shake their heads and say, "We have nothing to do with you guys. What? You killed in my name? You fought in my name? This is not what I came with." Every single one of them, if you read their writings, if you read their beautiful stories, wanted to bring peace. They wanted to bring love to people. They didn't want to bring the sword. We bring the sword, in their names, and they have nothing to do with that.

All three scriptures — of the Jews and Christians and Muslims — ratify what I say. They prove what I say. They all say that Moses, Jesus, and Mohammad brought love. That's all they are about. But we, their followers, are anything but that.

Odeh Muhawesh spent the first 18 years of his life living in Jordan and now lives in the United States. In his own words, he was a Middle Easterner and is now a Midwesterner. He travels often and has visited four continents.

Odeh believes that deep down we are all the same. If you put John Doe from a Western nation and Abdullah Mohammad from a Middle Eastern nation together in a room and they got to know each other, they would find that they both have the same fears and the same dreams. In his view, it is imperative that we get to know one another if we are going to get along in this world.

16

Marge Sullivan

To me, peace is where people can get along and be open to each other and try to understand each other.

Quite a few years ago, I was walking down Nicollet Mall and there was a man standing on the corner in front of a store. He was reaching out his hand saying, "Hello, how are you?" to everybody that went by. He wanted to shake somebody's hand and I, along with everybody else, walked right by this man. So I went a couple blocks and then I turned around and went back. He reached out his hand again and he said, "Hi, how are you?" And I said, "I'm great. How are you today?" And he said, "Fine." I said, "It's so nice you're out here shaking hands with everybody." And he said, "I just thought it'd be a nice thing to do today." I said, "You know I think it's a nice thing to do today, too."

I felt like something was guiding me, something in my heart said, "reach out." There was just something about the way he was doing it, too. He was trying hard. He was giving a gift to me and I wanted to give it back. So after that, I'd get on an elevator and I'd say, "Hi, how's everybody today?" Well, very seldom you'd get an answer, but every once in a while there would be a few who would say, "Good. I'm doing great." It just felt good, and I think it would feel good to the whole world if we could do more of that — to love your brothers and sisters and listen to each other.

Marge Sullivan is a volunteer at Peace House Community, a gathering place for homeless people and others in an urban neighborhood. Marge believes that we shouldn't judge each other so harshly, and that the world would be a better place if we could just learn to be more accepting of one another.

She says that as we get older, we begin to understand that we need to accept other people's differences. But since we aren't going to be around forever, if we are going to open our eyes, we had better open them wide and open them quickly.

18

PHOTOGRAPHED 5/14/2009

Gopal Khanna

20

Peace Corps is the country's most preeminent soft arm. One that seeks to bring America's peace and friendship to the world. As I look back at my time of service, I recognize that our nation was violated on 9/11. We, as a nation, were concerned first and foremost about our own security. When that happened, we were consumed with protecting ourselves, our assets, our interests, and our homeland.

President Bush had the foresight to recognize that while military operations were key to neutralize the terrorist elements that were looking to destabilize our nation, it was equally important to share America's good will and peace. During our time, the Peace Corps had 8,000 plus volunteers working in 72 countries, and had the highest level of budget in 30 years. It is probably one of the best-kept secrets in terms of politics and public policy.

We have volunteers serving in the remotest sections in Africa, in South America, in eastern European countries. And because they serve the communities and live with the communities, they become part of the communities. That's a very enriching experience for our volunteers and the communities, because they see firsthand what America and Americans are all about, because even people living abroad have a flawed notion of who we are as a people and what we are as a nation. When our people live and work with communities, they see us as good people, people who have noble ideas, who want to do good. And most important of all, that we are a very diverse, pluralistic, secular nation.

Gopal Khanna served as chief information officer for the state of Minnesota. Prior to that, he served as chief information officer and chief financial officer for the Peace Corps in the administration of President George W. Bush.

Gopal believes that the world is multi-polar and that we as individuals are multi-polar as well. Within each of us there is a combination of both good and evil. The most important path to finding peace is to find equilibrium in our own minds in order to balance conflicting thoughts and emotions.

PHOTOGRAPHED 9/29/2009

Jennifer McNally

I went to Florida to visit a dear friend of mine who had lung cancer. She's a person who has taught me a lot about centering myself and letting the noise and the chaos do their thing, but keeping it one step away from what's centered in my life. She was very sick. I drove straight from the airport to the hospital. She was in the hospital and she was not very coherent. There was a chart in her room that said the doctor's name and the nurse's name and what medications she was on. Then it said "patient goals," and it was blank.

She said, "Can you get me a pen? There's no patient goal listed, and I need to have a goal." And I wrote her goals: Get well. Go home. Spread joy. She was so concerned about giving to others . . . Even when she was so sick, she wanted to still be giving to others.

And I think finding that beauty — amidst so much pain — I'm going to remember that for the rest of my life. And when something's happening to me that seems terrible, if I can't be thinking of my friend saying she wanted to spread joy when she's in her hospital bed hardly able to breathe . . . if I can't keep that in mind, then there's something wrong with me.

That's what peace is to me . . . finding that kind of beauty. Even when there's pain, it's knowing that even when life is bad, it's still really, really good.

22

Jennifer McNally is a lawyer, wife, and mother of three. She believes that we are all connected on some level, and when something bad happens in the world, it affects us all. She uses meditation to quiet her heart and to find calmness amidst life's chaos.

Melvin Carter Jr.

If I would just come up with my own definition [of peace] right here and now, I think it's people living harmoniously with one another. And when I think about harmoniously — maybe melodically, maybe rhythmically — [I mean] together in ways where we can accept one another's idiosyncratics . . . And it probably wouldn't take much to figure out that you and I may have some beliefs that are just in opposition to one another. But when you think about us kind of living together symphonically . . . well, you know, in the symphony, you've got all kinds of stuff happening — rhythmically and melodically and harmoniously — at the same time. [Yet the instruments work] together in such a way that doesn't clash. You know, the bass will be the bass, and the trinkets will be the trinkets.

A retired St. Paul police officer, Melvin Carter Jr. works with Save Our Sons, an organization he helped found to mentor African American youth who are in trouble.

Melvin refers to his time on the police force as a calling. He viewed himself as a "peace" officer, and says he went into the "peacehood" much the same way a preacher or a minister goes into the ministry.

I mean, I thank God that we're all different. Man, as exciting of a person as I think I am, I think if everybody in this whole world was just a bunch of [Melvins], we'd be bored to tears. Man, I love to look at somebody who's just extremely different from me and go, "What?" I love to do that. And I'm sure people do the same when they look at me and when they listen to me. We can recognize and celebrate one another's uniqueness.

24

PHOTOGRAPHED 5/18/2009

Jeff Blodgett

I would look at the idea of peace on two levels: a big macro level and then on an individual, personal level. On the big level, I think peace can be achieved through the functioning and the maturing of real democratic (small "d" democratic) governing and systems. The peaceful transition of power, for instance, is something that we take for granted here in the United States, but it is something that doesn't happen in a lot of places and often involves lots of conflict and actual war and death and destruction.

On the personal level — I'm talking about peace from a political perspective — I would say peace comes from mature and genuine and skilled leaders. The basic definition of a leader is someone who's able to move people to action, and that is such an important skill and so required in our society and in a functioning democracy. It's about power. Power is usually wielded by leaders, and power is a neutral concept. Power can be used for good or evil.

Jeff Blodgett is executive director of Wellstone Action, an organization created to carry on the legacy of the late Senator Paul Wellstone and his wife, Sheila Wellstone. Jeff first met Paul Wellstone when he was a student in one of Wellstone's political science classes, and eventually he wound up serving as his campaign manager for each of his senate races.

The mission of Wellstone Action is to ignite the leadership in people and the power in communities to create progressive change.

Mature leaders understand the power that's in their hands to move people to action, and responsible, mature leaders are ones that use that leadership for good and help move people in a direction that leads to positive change in their lives and in society's lives. It has a lot to do with the ability to listen well to people, to understand where another person is coming from . . . so, the idea of empathy. Ultimately, people want to be heard and they want to be valued . . . they want to feel a part of something, and a good leader will make that happen for their followers. That, to me, is one of the building blocks of a peaceful interaction with individuals.

26

Morgan Murphy

I studied in South Africa for six months. I had a friend who's black and he obviously could have had so much hatred built up towards a lot of people in South Africa. But instead, the way that he would talk . . . was just so inspiring because he truly wanted to start fresh and have an understanding — a complete understanding — for the other. He said, "We are all South Africans," and that is the mentality that so many people have down there.

Morgan Murphy is a student at Loras College in Dubuque, Iowa, where she studies secondary education, history, and social sciences. Recently she returned from a six-month term studying in South Africa.

Morgan is a part of the peace and social justice community at Loras. She and her housemates in the Peace and Social Justice House organize discussions and other events to try to build awareness on campus of various issues.

Morgan is hopeful that we can become a more peaceful society, but she recognizes that in order to do so we have to be willing to recognize our own shortcomings.

We are all one body, we are all South Africans, we are all the same people. There's no racial difference anymore and so stop putting that in your head. That's the message that he wanted to send to everybody: Stop building these barriers that are not here anymore.

I think that that's something we can do in our own lives, too. There are so many times we put up these barriers, whether its religious barriers, racial barriers, and we talk about it in schools and we teach it to our kids, and it's like, why are we still talking about these barriers that are here? They can be broken down if we do it within our hearts.

PHOTOGRAPHED 1/29/2010

Luyen Phan

Peace is an absence of war. In the past 35 years, there have been very few periods of peace. People said that what happened in Nazi Germany wouldn't happen again, and then it did, in Cambodia and Darfur. The cynical side of me says that peace is a dream. It's great to live for and hope for, but we don't learn from history.

We get greedy. We want something we don't have, or more of what we already have. It's human nature. There are good people in the world, but sometimes there may not be enough of us to balance things out. Or we may not have enough real power — political, economic, cultural, linguistic, social — to stop these things.

As an international student adviser, my role is to have students from all over the world meet each other, to promote understanding rather than fear and intolerance. The kids here are from various cultural and religious backgrounds, but they care for and support each other, and they speak up when they feel that someone is mistreating their friend.

Whether we are fortunate enough to visit another country, or meet someone in our own country who is an immigrant, a refugee, or even a high school exchange student, we can get to know people from other parts of the world. Small exchanges can grow into deeper discussions. Hopefully, over time, those relationships continue to build. It may be years or decades later, but when we read a story about a place and whatever bad thing is happening there, we will think about our friend who is from there, or about the student who went back there. I believe those small experiences will help people work toward some sort of world peace.

30

Luyen Phan was born in Vietnam and his family moved to the United States during the final days of the war, when he was six years old. A Lutheran church in Redwood Falls, Minnesota, sponsored Phan's family, and his parents have lived in that town for 35 years.

With a Fulbright scholarship, Luyen studied in Singapore and went on to work in Thailand. Today he works with international students and believes that student exchange programs can lay a valuable foundation for understanding and accepting different cultures.

PHOTOGRAPHED 2/12/2010

Mark Williams

Eighty percent of the world's energy currently is produced by fossil fuels, which are a limited resource. Further, fossil fuels — combusted in the typical way we do it — produce carbon dioxide. It has become obvious that we have to move away from them.

We have to meet people's legitimate needs for energy while we keep the planet from going bust as a consequence. This is one of the hardest things that humanity has ever faced. It's a global problem, and the mechanisms for adjudicating things on a global scale are not strong. Without the right governance in place to allocate resources and manage costs, we face the potential for tragedy on a global scale.

With regard to peace, if developing people's needs aren't met, tensions will increase on a global scale. If global warming goes forward unabated, its effects will be felt unequally and create conflict. If nation-states focus on supplying their own security, when we finally pay the price for global warming, it will be much more difficult and much more expensive. There are no simple solutions. Exercising leadership, thinking about next steps, the next source of energy, and the next source of wealth and mobility, are important because it takes decades to change these systems.

Ideas about proper governance, the role of the state, individual responsibility — all of this is converging. You can point to examples where that isn't happening, but overall the pattern is quite powerful. The world is growing up, and we are thinking about the right way to underpin a peaceful society.

Mark Williams is downstream director for Royal Dutch Shell, which means he oversees refining, marketing, trading, chemicals, logistics — every step involved in getting crude oil to the consumer. Shell provides about 10 percent of the world's fuel supply.

Mark recognizes the environmental challenges we face with our dependence on fossil fuels, but he defends energy production as fundamental to prosperity and peace in the world.

32

PHOTOGRAPHED 2/10/2010

33

Hudlin Wagner

When we talk about peace, we think about war. But we have to begin in our own land, in our own families, even in our own lives. Integrating the discussion of peace into our lives early on through our learning systems would help us consistently envision peace as achievable. Instead, our society has romanticized warriors: Genghis Khan, the Zulus, the Iroquois.

I believe in the goodness of human beings. A large percentage of people around the world do share a deep desire for peace, but we don't often exercise a means of achieving it.

Hudlin Wagner says that her perceptions of peace are a result of her tri-cultural background. She is black, Native American, and West Indian. Hudlin defines peace initially as a physical feeling — a lightness of being, which includes a spiritual connection with the world and its order.

When Hudlin was a young girl, her parents decided that she should attend the local Catholic school. As the first student of color to attend the school, she found that none of the children would sit near her because they were afraid that her skin color would rub off on them if she touched them. When she asked her parents to send her to a different school, they told her, "This is your journey to be introduced to each individual human being — so you don't recreate the stereotypes of every race."

I'm hopeful because I'm seeing more and more individuals step forward. Neutrality won't be an option. We are living in a time when the impact of not working together for peace leaves us only the alternative of destruction. We need to hear from the leadership of the next generation coming up around the world. We're ready for it. We are accustomed to thinking about addictions as abusive and destructive. I would love to live in a society with people who are addicted to peace. Wouldn't that be one hell of an addiction?

34

PHOTOGRAPHED 2/18/2010

Eric Gibson

In Buddhism, we make a very clear distinction between peace [that] comes from the outside and peace [that] comes from the inside. And oftentimes, historically, if you look at the development of societies, there's many times when there is peace in society where you wouldn't have wanted to be a part of it, because it was peace that came from a sword or something of that nature. It's peaceful as long as you don't do this, this, or this.

Buddhism works more on an inner level. You can say Buddhism is a method or religion or practice that specializes in finding happiness. And generally, when you're able to realize that actually everybody wants to be happy, it's kind of a common denominator for all beings, humans and otherwise. And so all of a sudden you realize that it's hard to separate your own wish for happiness from the wish for happiness for all beings.

36

Eric Gibson is a Buddhist teacher who travels the globe teaching in different countries and cultures. He credits those Buddhist teachings with helping him understand that we are all connected.

Eric talks about the flawed model that if we gather all the perfect elements — the perfect career, the perfect partner, the perfect home in the perfect neighborhood — we will be happy.

There's a funny Buddhist saying: "If you think about your own happiness, you always have problems. And if you think about the happiness of others, then there's always interesting work to do." So in this way, by focusing really more on helping all beings find happiness, as a side effect you naturally find happiness yourself. And with happiness comes a lot of inner peace.

Rabbi Amy Eilberg

I definitely do not always get this right. You can ask my family, my colleagues. I've been living and breathing these questions for years now, and I regularly blurt out an ill-thought response to someone articulating something they believe which is very different from something that is important to me.

I hope that I'm getting better at it. It helps when I'm prepared. When I know that I'm sitting with a Palestinian leader, if I'm bringing an interfaith group to listen to Israeli peacemakers, when I'm moving into a situation which is, by definition, going to be conflictual.

I'm likely to do some conscious breathing. I remind myself to slow down the pace of my communication, to slow down the pace of my reaction time, to open up a space between the time when I'm inwardly reacting and when I'm responding. Sometimes it's whispering to myself to just listen. Sometimes it's consciously watching my breath as someone is talking and I feel my pulse beginning to beat more rapidly. I remind myself to notice that the stillness is gone from my mind, and my body, and my spirit.

Sometimes such moments, when they're really hard and challenging, are enlivening, because there's a sort of wordless sense within me that this is when you get to be present for one of these moments that are potentially moments of conflict, but might also hold the possibility of a peaceful encounter.

Rabbi Amy Eilberg is the first woman to be ordained by the Conservative Movement of Judaism. She spent the early part of her rabbinate in grief counseling and end-of-life care, but focuses her work today on peace and reconciliation.

Amy spends much of her time on interfaith dialogue. She believes that peace does not come from avoiding the difficult issues, but by facing them directly and having honest, respectful dialogue about our differences.

The foundation of her peace work is a 40-year history of Jewish prayer and a 20-year practice of meditation in which she cultivates the still places within, while striving to become aware of those places that remain unsettled.

38

Jamal Hashi

You know, the Bible, the Qur'an, they all give the same message. But people fight about who was the messenger. The core of the message is: achieve peace, give peace, and live by peace. But what do we fight about? The difference of who was the messenger. It's like killing the mailman because he wasn't the same mailman last week. Did you get the mail? That's all that matters.

Upon my 27-year journey on this planet, experiencing my three lives — that's what we should call it — the moment I experienced true peace is actually right now, at this moment. How so? Because I have the free will to do anything and my worries are not threats for my life. I have the three greatest things that a human needs: shelter, food, and a person who loves me very dearly. I smile more than I used to. My facial muscles are stretched upwards, so I think now is when I am truly happy and I know what peace means. I know what it feels like. Before, I used to just guess what peace would be like or maybe imagine what it would be like, but today I think I've reached that moment. I travel at free will. I have no boss. I do as I please. I wake up whenever I want to. I go to bed whenever I want to. My fridge is full and my stomach is full. I am very comfortable and happy where I am at right now. I think this is, to me, peace.

Born in Somalia, Jamal Hashi was in elementary school there when the war began. It sounded like thunder, he said. He fled with his older brother, taking refuge with family friends, and making their way to the southern part of the country, where eventually they snuck onto a ship filled with refugees who were escaping the war.

Jamal now lives in the United States, where he owns and operates a restaurant. He says he has lived three lives: a stable childhood in Somalia, a coming-of-age stage during the chaos and uncertainty of the war, and his current life in the United States. He feels fortunate to be in America, where he has found a life of peace, because he experienced a complete absence of peace during his earlier years.

40

41

Al Quie

There was not peace in my one-room school. The kids rebelled against the teacher and I refused to rebel with them, so I was ostracized. Dad took me out of that school and put me in a four-room school. I was damaged emotionally enough so that I didn't know how to make friends. The teacher probably noticed that and she said, "Albert, if you will stay in for the noon hour, I will tutor you, because you're behind the other kids." I was just too scared to try and make friends with the others. That was a way out, and she tutored me well enough that I excelled. That's a part of peace, where you look at a person and see there's something that you can help them with.

The first thing you do is meet people where they are. There is fear to make that step — to reach out. And if I reach out, there can be fear to reach back again. When we do that, something starts developing. But somebody has to leave their comfort zone. That means those with the greatest confidence in who they are before God, or the most educated, and those who assume positions of leadership need to do that, because there are broken hurting people who desperately need a friend and need safety. You can't expect them to do that. But if you reach out, not only do you build a relationship, but you become enlightened as well.

42

Al Quie served as the 35th governor for Minnesota, from 1979 through 1983, and he currently is working on several governmental initiatives as well as with Prison Fellowship ministries.

Al doesn't believe that we can ever achieve world peace because of our competing political, economic, and belief systems. He believes the broken human condition will prevent us from achieving total peace.

But Al believes in working toward inner peace and peace within communities. He explores the idea that broken people are not in a place where they can reach out to others, and it is the obligation of those of us who are better off to reach out to our brothers and sisters who are struggling.

43

The McDonald Sisters

Jane: I try to invest my energy and my consciousness to be aware of what makes peace, and it does start very close to the soul. When you get in touch with your own soul . . . heart and mind are at peace. It can be just as contagious and addictive as violence.

Brigid: Once you've established the horrors of war and the horrors of terrible fights and how mean people can be to one another, you recognize that peace must start within. I think we need to learn to communicate peacefully . . . start learning the words that bring about peace instead of agitating.

Rita: I go on what my conscience tells me and awakens me to and then I'm out there trying to do something about it. I have very little hope that anything will change because people have been hoping for generation after generation that things will change, and greed is still here, stronger than ever, and that moves into violence. But I know I live in my own hope that I will do what I can to counteract that evil, and that's my responsibility.

Kate: We have about 26 nephews and nieces. I know we've had an influence in their lives in the sense that they know what we're doing. They see what we're involved in and you can't get away from that issue. Some children grow up, probably don't see any demonstrations or really aren't seeing anything publicly that would get their consciousness. But I think that [our nephews and nieces] are going to be very aware of working for peace and speaking up for peace.

Opposite page, left to right; Jane, Brigid, Kate, and Rita McDonald are four biological sisters who joined the order of St. Joseph of Carondelet and also became Catholic Sisters.

Raised on a farm in western Minnesota, they found a richness growing up close to the earth and learned about community from watching their extended family help one another on a daily basis.

All four of them are active in peace and justice issues, and all four of them have spent time in jail for nonviolent actions they have taken because of their beliefs.

44

PHOTOGRAPHED 7/31/2009

Richard Rittmaster

In working with the soldiers, my goal is always to help them integrate some of the scary things that they experience so those events don't become the central, defining aspects of who they are, but that there is something beyond that . . . something deeper, more profound, and life-giving. And as I've been able to do that in one-on-one conversations, small groups, or in the course of a Sunday morning worship service . . . what I've discovered is that they begin to see themselves and what they are doing in a different way. When you start to lower the anxiety and the fear, it allows people to be more thoughtful in terms of how they interact with local nationals or the contract workers from other countries. And it creates an environment where people see each other as human beings. When you create opportunities where people can see each other as individuals, it lessens the possibility that all these folks who are walking around with guns are going to actually pick them up and use them against each other.

I talk to a lot of soldiers who have been traumatized by their experiences. They have been on multiple deployments. I've taken the machine guns out of their hands, because the concern was that they were going to do violence to themselves.

What we want to constantly do is create opportunities where people can see beyond the immediacy of their own suffering, to find that inner voice that speaks of wholeness and speaks of hope . . . a purposefulness to their life. Those kinds of experiences, especially in a combat zone, are the kinds of things that are going to contribute to less violence and more possibility for peace.

46

Richard Rittmaster served as family life chaplain for the 34th Infantry Division in Basra, Iraq. After working for many years as a congregational pastor in the Lutheran church, Rick joined the military, knowing he would be shipped into a war zone.

Rick chose this path, not because he has an appetite for war, but rather because he has a passion for helping broken people through difficult times.

He explored ways to diffuse tensions in volatile situations and how to find a personal, authentic, inner peace amidst strife.

Flora Tsukayama

I went to school — preschool all the way to senior high — in Japan. I'm Japanese, but I'm an American. I was born just 6 years after World War II, so a lot of my classmates' parents fought in the war against the Japanese, so there were a lot of slurs that I heard while I was growing up. On the military base, my classmates who were Caucasian and African American looked down on the Japanese and it was tough for me to be there, hearing slurs all the time. You just have to continue. I can only imagine what my father went through, working as a civil servant, working for the military, but on a smaller scale I was facing that in school.

So, when I came here, I looked at the population in Minnesota and it was predominantly white and fears came back again. I wanted to protect my children. World War II was so far away that I knew nothing like that would happen, but there is always fear as a parent. So I decided to volunteer in school, and if my children needed me, I'd be there. If anybody had any questions about our background or our culture, I could be there to explain it. Although I am an American, I wanted to be an ambassador — a positive person to teach positive things, and so I taught a lot of Japanese culture, crafts, and origami.

I just want the school environment to be safe. You can't educate anybody if they are worried or scared. Peace is when you have a peace of mind. You can be happy inside and outside — I think that's when you have peace.

Flora Tsukayama was born in Tokyo, Japan, six years after the end of World War II. Flora's father was a Japanese American who lived in Hawaii when Pearl Harbor was bombed. He immediately enlisted in the U.S. military and worked as a translator, eventually moving to Tokyo in order to assist the reconstruction effort. Flora's mother was a Japanese citizen.

Flora attended a school for U.S. dependents in Tokyo, where she often felt unwelcome due to her Japanese heritage, and endured frequent racial slurs and negative comments directed toward her. Today Flora is a full-time volunteer in the public school system. She provides an adult presence in a hallway that was once notorious for bullying. Her time, attention, and compassion have helped turn that hallway into a more civil and open place.

48

PHOTOGRAPHED 2/4/2010

Michael Kiesow Moore

I experience peace most through creativity: through writing, sometimes through art, through music and dance. When I am being creative, I feel like I am really accessing what peace is all about in my own sense of inner peace.

I was beset by bullies throughout my entire growing up, and throughout that whole time, I refused to fight. I would just not fight bullies or be engaged in fighting. It was almost like every cell in my body was programmed to go the route of nonviolence. It's like it was a part of my being. The one time in middle school when I did choose to fight back, it was definitely the wrong thing to do and almost from that moment on, I just decided, okay, I am not going there again. It wasn't that I came away physically bruised, though I did, but it was more that I was going against my own internal convictions. And when I realized that I was going against what I personally believed, against my own ethics . . . that was what was so wrong and I absolutely could not ever want to do that again.

And you know, I don't think the distance from a bully's fist to that of the arsenal of a nation is really that far. I think it's all part of the same kind of construct.

Michael Kiesow Moore teaches a class he calls "Writing Peace into the World." He uses writing as a tool for exploring what we know about peace and as a method for accessing peace in our own lives.

For Michael, the creative process leads to peace. He has helped coordinate public readings that focus on peace and a festival called Art of Peace.

Michael believes we need to bring peace into our lives in small ways, because these small steps can ripple to larger issues.

50

PHOTOGRAPHED 5/27/2009

Catherine Mamer

When I came [to Peace House] 22 years ago, I realized that I had something to learn. I was out there in the streets, fighting for peace, and working on committees and boards, trying to change everything in the world. But I realized that I hadn't really gotten it. You just have to *be*. You just have to trust that what you have in you innately will be enough for the person you're with. And so you sit down and you say, "Hi, how are you doing today? Would you like a cup of coffee? Do you have anything you want to talk about? I'm not having such a good day today. How is your day going? Isn't the sunshine wonderful?" So little. It's that simple and that hard. Peace means so many different things to me, but basically, peace is being able to have an environment where you feel safe.

52

Catherine Mamer is the co-director of Peace House Community, a gathering place that she says, "offers a place of hospitality for people who generally don't feel welcomed in other places. We come to meet whoever walks in our door, without judgment."

Catherine recognizes that simple acts of kindness and understanding can go far to provide healing for those who have rarely experienced such things.

She talks about changing the world one person at a time, even if that person is yourself.

Everybody has a struggle with something. We get so angry. Life comes in and devastates us. Our children die, our parents die, our best friends die. The people we rely upon get sick and we have to take care of them.

Our houses burn down and we lose so much. We lose connection with our families and we're angry. We're hurt. We don't know how to get through that struggle, and we don't have many people to help us if we don't pick ourselves up by our bootstraps. The first thing that we do at Peace House is to try to calm the anger and try to find some peace.

53

V. David Schwantes

We really have a whole new set of circumstances today than we did even 50 years ago, yet we retain the same ideologies, the same mindsets, the same beliefs and attitudes as though there'd been no change at all. So to begin a discussion about peace in our time, with the notion that nothing much is going to change and that our ideas and our policies and our philosophies are appropriate for the future, is to be in error. We have to start from the premise that there's going to be a lot of change, accelerating change, and we're going to have to have new words on a clean piece of paper in order to deal effectively with that.

It was easier to live well together when there were 1.6 billion people here in the world. We weren't running into each other as much. When there's 10 or 12 billion people in the world, it's going to be a whole lot more face-to-face, nose-to-nose, and we'd better learn how to get along.

V. David Schwantes is an author whose latest book is titled *Finding Happiness With Truth, Beauty and Ethics.* In his book, he talks about how our society looks at life through an economic and a political lens. David writes that if we are going to survive this century, we need to begin looking at life through a different lens — an ethical lens.

He describes the challenges we'll face as our global population reaches more than 10 billion people by 2050. And though he has grave concerns related to inflated military spending and global economic imbalances, in the end, he has hope in the basic goodness of individuals.

Peace to me is a matter of living well and living well together, and that means an energization of core values, universal core values of respect, of fairness, of decency, of empathy, of sharing. And it's an absence of exploitation. It's an absence of violence, of hatred, and of gross inequity. It is not a total elimination of fault lines, because our human condition will never eliminate all of the things that separate us, but it is instead more of a preoccupation with *us* rather than a preoccupation with *me*.

Imani Jaafar-Mohammad

I do presentations about women's rights in Islam. Like, "What's the Islamic view on a woman's place in Islam?" It's a very egalitarian religion and I don't think people understand that, so I've had times where I've given these two-hour presentations and I'll have some guy stand up and say, "Well, I think you are so oppressed." And I'm like, "You don't even know me."

So I think hearing those comments, especially when I first started doing this, was really hard. But now I'm just kind of used to it and I know how to deal with it. But I feel like if there is one person that walks away from that and says, "Thanks for the information, I think it will really be helpful" . . . that's worth it.

Imani Jaafar-Mohammad is a lawyer and partner in a law firm with her husband. Born in the United States to Lebanese immigrants, she feels she has acted as a peace broker for most of her life, both formally and informally.

Imani speaks often to school, business, and church groups in an effort to help people understand what it means to be a Muslim woman in America today. She encourages people to get their information firsthand and not accept stereotypes about other cultures and religions.

You are going to have those people that just don't want to learn anything, and I've learned that you just have to leave them. Maybe one day something will click and it will change, but otherwise you just focus on the people that want to learn. I feel like I learn from people, too. I went once to a church . . . an ice cream social with a bunch of 70-year-old women and they were in a Lutheran church. I have not known very many Lutherans in my life until I moved to Minnesota, and so I asked them all these questions about their church, and they got an opportunity to teach me something I didn't know. I feel like that's how you do it, but not everyone's willing to do that, and that's been a huge obstacle.

56

57

Mel Duncan

I have seen things that I would rather not see and would rather not know. I have seen horrific things done to people. Yet if we are going to engage and transform, that exposure [and] that deep knowledge is required. I continue to believe that when most of us are presented with those kinds of conditions, we will act to change those conditions. I think that it's a situation of keeping one's heart open so it can be broken and broken again. If it's not open . . . if there are not those cracks, there is not the space for active compassion. And that active compassion, based upon a true understanding of the realities of this world . . . not some romanticized notion but the true understandings of the struggles, open one to the possibilities of how we work to change.

We struggle with a shrunken notion of our own ability. We have the ability to bring substantial change and often we don't own that. We are afraid of that. In fact, we can bring change and it often comes from a very small group of dedicated and persistent people. We have many examples in history of that.

Courage is living and working amid violence with nonviolence as your only tool . . . with people who have given up the illusion of the gun. To be active nonviolent peacekeepers requires great courage. Sometimes analysts will talk about peace being weakness, but most of the military people we encounter who see our work in the field have great respect. Interestingly, many of the military people that we work with are very interested in finding nonviolent alternatives because they have seen the blood, and most people don't like it.

58

Mel Duncan is executive director of Nonviolent Peaceforce, a well-trained, unarmed peacekeeping force that works in regions of violent conflict around the world to protect local peacemakers.

Even in the most violent places on earth, Mel says there are creative and courageous people doing amazing things to foster peace, and it is Nonviolent Peaceforce's mission to create the space for those local people to do their peacebuilding work safely.

PHOTOGRAPHED 5/29/2009

Rev. Andre Golike

Peace for me is when you work, you come back to your house, you sleep. Tomorrow you wake up, and you go on your way. There is not something you fear. You feel yourself, you feel happy, you meet with people . . . you talk about your own life, life of the people, the country. As for us Christians, we talk about the church, freely. That is what I can see as peace.

In our country we are not rich enough, but we are not hungry because everybody can farm, and take food from his farm, and then cook and eat. When people come together, though they are not rich, you see how people are excited to thank their God. From the other side . . . those who are wealthy can ask, "Oh, how can those people thank God about their situation?" But they know that they're healthy, they are not sick, and they have their daily food. That's enough. So they thank God for that instead of looking for more that they are not able to get.

Rev. Andre Golike is president of the Evangelical Lutheran Church in Central African Republic (CAR). I spoke with him when he visited Minneapolis to build support for his ministry.

With an average annual income of $410, the people of CAR face many challenges. But despite this lack of material resources, Andre finds a wealth of joy in the people and great hope in the promise of people working together toward a common goal.

Our former president said if a man is alone, then he will be a suffering man. But when we come together as a society, as a community, then he will get a better life. So I hope that together, if we plan for a better life, then we will get there.

I think that most of what we long for as peace is inner peace. When you trust yourself, and you are confident in yourself, I think this is the best you can have as peace in the world.

60

Barbara Nordstrom-Loeb

Sometimes when people say *peace,* it's sort of masking differences. A lot of stuff gets marginalized if everything's just all nice-nice. Everybody gets along, but it's at the sacrifice of the ways that people are different and sometimes do bump up against each other.

For me, peace is a place where everything is represented and welcomed and present. And that's much more complicated, because then you have to figure out, "How do I relate to, or accept, or be with other parts that I don't like or don't want or wish they would go away?" You have the right to your beliefs, but you don't have the right to impose them on me or on anyone else, and each one of us has to figure out how do we relate to someone else's beliefs that we really disagree with.

Barbara Nordstrom-Loeb is a psychotherapist, an educator, and a healer. She is involved with many social action issues, including Jewish peace work related to Israel and Palestine.

Barbara views fear as an obstacle to peace and recalls a parable told by a Native American elder. Two wolves are engaged in a battle inside each of us. One wolf represents peace, hope, and truth, while the second wolf represents fear, anger, and lies. When asked which wolf would win, the man replied, "The one you feed."

A client recently said, "You mean I don't have to like everybody?" No! I don't think anybody does. You get to say, "This is somebody I don't want to spend too much time with." Doesn't mean they're bad. Doesn't mean you're bad. It's about accepting yourself, too.

I think about buying clothes. [People say] always have a beige shirt, because beige goes with everything. At some point I thought, "The last thing in the world I want to be is beige. Why would I want to get along with everybody?" If the only way I could get along with everybody in the world is by being beige, I don't want to. I want to be the rough and funky parts of me, and the wonderful parts of me, and I think that is hopefully true of everybody.

62

63

Jack Nelson-Pallmeyer

I think we need this fundamental reassessment of what military power is and isn't good for. For the most part, I think the role of a military should be to defend one's borders, not to defend an imperial reach. We have more than 750 permanent military bases outside of our borders. We have hundreds of thousands of troops. Most of our preparation isn't for national defense, it's for power projection, and that undermines peace rather than enhances peace.

When you have overwhelming superiority in military power, almost all the problems you face will be defined through a military lens. Every time we militarize we accelerate the pace of our economic decline. Dwight Eisenhower said that every gun we make, every warship we launch, is ultimately a theft from the poor and the hungry. But it's also a theft from our middle class schools. It's a theft from our nonexistent public transit system. There are no military solutions to hunger and poverty. There are no military solutions to climate change. There are no military solutions to terrorism. Terrorism is a tactic. One of the most costly decisions ever made in this country was a decision to respond to the terrorist attacks of 9/11 with a war on terror, rather than to see it as an international crime that needed to be dealt with by finding people, bringing them to justice, and by preventing them from doing what they're doing.

Jack Nelson-Pallmeyer is an associate professor who teaches justice and peace studies at the University of St. Thomas in St. Paul. He has written more than a dozen books, and spent years studying issues of poverty and hunger and how they relate to peace and social justice in our world.

In 2008 Jack ran for the DFL party nomination for one of Minnesota's U.S. Senate seats, a nomination he eventually lost to Al Franken.

64

PHOTOGRAPHED 1/29/2010

Khant Khant Kyaw

I was born Buddhist. My grandma is very religious, so I was exposed to Buddhism when I was young through folklore and temple visits. When we moved to Singapore, I lost that connection. I don't have a sound foundation of Buddhism yet, but it's something that I've started exploring again. There are three Buddhist principles that I live by to foster peace within myself. The first is awareness, the second is understanding, and the third is contentment. Awareness is being open and having the ability to communicate in terms of expressing oneself as well as listening — knowing where someone else comes from.

Tolerance or understanding happens on a deeper level when you try to gain an insight into the other person's perspective, and perhaps even embrace it if that resonates within you.

Contentment says, "Follow the middle path or the middle way." Giving in to your desires too much is not a good thing because you'll be overwhelmed. Being content is a remedy to console yourself when you don't get something that you want. That may stop you from engaging in negative actions or words that could promote conflict.

Is it our responsibility to promote peace globally? How far should we go? As a 22-year-old woman, I would say to do whatever makes you happy without making others unhappy. A simple answer to a very complex question.

Khant Khant Kyaw is a recent college graduate with a degree in international studies. She was born in Burma (officially known as the Union of Myanmar) but she lived in Singapore for 10 years while she was growing up. In 2010 she received a $10,000 Davis Project for Peace grant to use community photography as a tool for the education and development of youth in Burma.

Khant Khant defines peace on many levels, from the international peace she hopes to foster with her future career to the inner peace she finds shaped by her Buddhist upbringing.

66

PHOTOGRAPHED 2/22/2010

Rev. Harry Wendt

What the advertising world wants us to do is to submit to this notion that we are here to buy things we don't need with money we don't have to impress people who do not care. Or take it a step further: we're here to make what we can, can what we make, and sit on the lid. This philosophy prevails and it's causing great problems around the world because the focus is on self rather than on the world as community.

Well, it's very difficult for us little human beings who live on this atom of an earth to understand the full sweep of history and to understand the implications of living on this little planet . . . so it goes on and the whole goal of life is to accumulate goods and to enjoy them and to live comfortably.

The peace that Jesus is calling us to get involved in is to understand that we live on a planet we didn't make and don't own, we live in a body which we didn't make and don't own, and we are here to learn to walk in the steps of Jesus, as servants of God and each other. What would it be like on planet Earth if every person alive were to ask, "How can I use life to glorify God by serving others without any thought of borders, flags, and skin color?" We'd live in a completely different world.

Rev. Harry Wendt is an Australian citizen who has lived in the United States since 1976. He founded and continues to run an organization called Crossways International, which is dedicated to Christian education.

Harry holds up Jesus as a model for his belief that we should live a life of service to our fellow human beings. In a global history that is dominated by pursuit of empire, Harry says that we need to examine the world as it is today and ask ourselves if our actions are intended to dominate others, or to serve them?

68

69

Kelly Connole

A number of years ago I was teaching a seminary course called "Pottery and Proclamation." One woman had recently lost her partner to cancer and was mourning the loss of someone incredibly important to her. As she learned how to make pots, she decided it would be powerful for her to make a pot to hold her partner's ashes. There is an understanding in Native American cultures that you're making pots out of your ancestors. We all become part of the earth, so when that earth is used to make pots, the pots actually have bits of our ancestors. So she and I talked about sifting some of her partner's ashes into the clay to make the vessel that would then hold the rest of them. We decided to meet at Northern Clay Center to make this vessel in the middle of the day, because we thought it would be a quieter time. In fact, there was a children's class in the next room and we could hear their laughter.

Kelly Connole is an artist who teaches ceramics and metal smithing at Carleton College. In her ceramics classes, students participate in the Empty Bowls project, making hundreds of bowls, filling them with soup during a spring event on campus, and taking in donations that are passed along to local food shelves.

Kelly believes that clay has taught her more about generosity than anything else in her life. She says that if you have a skill, that skill can be used to be generous . . . and being generous is one step on the path toward peace.

While we listened to the noise of children, we sifted some of the ashes into the clay and threw a simple container on the wheel. The woman had only been working with clay for a few weeks, and it was as though the clay just threw itself, as though our hands were barely there. The vessel took shape in a wonderful, peaceful way. And now it's in her house — this container that is made of this person whom she loved so much.

To hear those children's voices while I was making a piece with someone whom I didn't know well, yet was sharing this intimate part of her life, I felt like, "Oh, this is peace. This is a perfect moment." Perfect in a messy, confusing, emotional sort of way, and I guess that that's what makes the most sense to me.

70

PHOTOGRAPHED 2/22/2010

Sami Rasouli

I'm an American-Iraqi citizen. I was born in Iraq in 1951. In 1986 I moved to the United States, where I ran a very successful business called Sinbad. It's a combination restaurant and bakery, and also we provided a line of Middle Eastern groceries and European products. So it was very nice — until the war broke out in 2003 and my dilemma began.

I am the American 100 percent waging the war against me, the Iraqi, 100 percent. So I was torn and tortured. I was not at peace. Then, when I decided to go back [to Iraq], I felt I am now at peace and I can deliver peace talks and reconciliation and explain to the Iraqis, my country people there, something went wrong when the first bullet flew on the night of the 19th of March, 2003.

Sami Rasouli is an Iraqi and an American citizen. He had been living in the United States for 17 years when the war broke out in 2003 and his dilemma began. He found he was both the invader and the invaded. After a brief trip to Iraq to reconnect with family, he decided to sell his possessions and move back to Iraq in 2004 to work on peace initiatives.

Sami founded the Muslim Peacemaker Teams in Iraq and works on a number of projects designed to diffuse tensions in that country, as well as projects that build connections between Iraqis and Americans.

Sami returns to America regularly to help build those connections and to speak about his work in Iraq.

A friend of mine described my decision to go back as a salmon up the stream. This friend reminded me that salmon don't come back. "But please," he said, "I want Sami to come back."

I committed myself to stay in Iraq five years to do work that would lead to a different kind of surge . . . not militarily, but doctors, engineers, and business people. Peace for me is stability, and when you are stable, the human development comes. Wars just impede the evolution of human beings.

72

Marlene Jezierski

When you're a child "peace on earth, good will to men" is a very abstract concept. It's what happens at Christmas time. My childhood experience was not outstanding, but as time went on, injustices started inserting themselves into my consciousness. And I suppose as you become closer to an age of reason, you start thinking, "That's wrong. There's something wrong with that."

There wasn't violence in my home when I was a child . . . but my father was very racist. And to me, that's a violent thing. Racism is violence. When I started teaching these classes . . . when I thought about what violence is, people would say, "Words are not violent." But we'd have discussions in the classes and [we realized that words can] do more damage than actions do.

The older I got, the harder it became for me to read about killing of any kind. I came to decide that there is no just war. I had to think about that a long time. [Now] I simply don't believe there is a just war. I can't believe it.

And so all the peace issues that are out there, I guess it's all just part of the same thing. You do what you can do, and my place . . . is to help people understand that words can hurt and damage, and we have to stop that.

I'll emphasize how important I think it is that the connection be made from the bottom up. Peace in the heart, peace in the home, peace in the neighborhood, and it goes up from there. And also how important it is that people recognize [the] part they can have in that [peace].

74

Marlene Jezierski spent more than 30 years as an emergency room nurse and, eventually, got involved in educating health care professionals about family violence.

Now retired, Marlene writes poetry about domestic abuse. She has published a book of her poems entitled *Beyond the Mirror,* in order to give victims skills, knowledge, encouragement, and support to help them see that they have choices available to them.

PHOTOGRAPHED 2/22/2010

75

David Harris

There's got to be internal peace. It's a matter of faith for me. It's not a matter of all reason. I should tell you I'm not Christian, I'm Jewish, but I've been a very strong lover of the teachings of Jesus, as I am of Gandhi and of Martin Luther King Jr. and many others. To me, the idea of peace has to include being at peace with one's self and that means being consistent. It means understanding the sources of violence — within your own person. I don't know about others, but I know there's plenty of violence in me that has lessened, but it's still there over the years. I can tell you a story.

We were in Minneapolis one cold winter night. We were walking down Hennepin Avenue going to a theater and a guy came walking by. He was a young man and he saw me and I must have looked like a Jew — whatever that is — because as he walked by, he just muttered, "I hate Jews." I turned around without even a thought — it was like a flash — and I said, "Fuck you, you son of a bitch." My wife took me by the elbow and we turned back and walked on.

I was mortified. Here I was talking and thinking increasingly about nonviolence and I had that in me, you know? I recognize the need to come to terms with myself and to be forgiving of others, because they're no different from me.

David Harris served in the U.S. Air Force as a surgeon during the Vietnam War. His objections to war and violence began with that conflict and eventually grew to include all wars. He is now a member of Veterans for Peace.

David believes that we all have violence within us, and only when we learn to address that tendency can we begin to hope for a broader peace.

Kim Smith

Peace in my life would be the state of complete oneness with everything, that sense of no conflict, no stress, and no strife. Complete ease. That includes love of myself, love of race, love of gender, class, occupation, family, and friends. Also I'd say peace with your appearance. I feel that especially in today's society, there's this push to have a certain look or to fit in a certain mold, but [you should] try to embrace yourself for who you are, and for what you look like, and really just praise that and love that. Every day I am just striving to find that place.

We talk a lot about peace and respecting everyone, but I think at a deeper level, we don't really trust each other. I think if we trusted each other, listened to each other, and didn't stereotype as much — which is easier said than done — I think in time by learning and knowing different types of people, the anger hopefully will dissipate and [our first response] would be the love.

I am hopeful for peace. I really do believe that listening to one another and trying to understand one another is a huge step towards peace because once you understand someone's point of view, whether you agree or not, you can work toward some kind of compromise or some sort of tolerance or at the minimum some kind of respect. And I think with that, true peace can begin.

I am hopeful. A lot has changed in the world. We still have a long ways to go, I think, but things are better.

Kim Smith is a writer, a poet and a rapper.

While she recognizes that many of today's commercial artists convey messages that are not peaceful, Kim's goal is to spread a message of love and acceptance through her music.

She believes that being patient with others and trying to connect in small ways with people on a daily basis can be the first steps toward creating a more peaceful world.

78

Chuck Hoffman

I see art bringing people together. Deeply seeded in all of us is God's imprint, and we have that creative spirit within us. There's a creative part of us that we really don't acknowledge or tap into, or it's just dismissed in our lives. We see it as frivolous. But Peg and I see it as another language that connects people in a profound and divine way. I believe that we go beyond our thinking, into our hearts, and there's some God connection that breaks through all the things that separate us. It has that kind of power. My heart sings when I get connected to that. I'm transformed. Time goes away and someplace in the midst of that, there's transformation and growth . . . seeing the world in a different way . . . seeing another person in a different way.

When we come up [against] people who we disagree with, we tend to move and try to find our tribe that agrees. We end up splintering into little boats on the sea, so to speak. We're all separate boats on this giant ocean and yet, there's more [to be gained from] drawing together, even though we're different.

Do we, as a culture, really want to understand and hear the other person or is it easier just to walk away? I've done both in my life and when I have stuck with something that was difficult to do, it always resulted in some sort of growth. If you can stick through some of it, it can lead to glimmers of peace and hope, but if you walk away completely, you really miss that opportunity.

80

Chuck Hoffman was artist-in-residence in 2010 at Luther Seminary in St. Paul. He and his wife, Peg Carlson-Hoffman, operate Genesis+Art Studio in Kansas City, Missouri.

Together they use art as a path to foster healing and reconciliation in areas of conflict. Groups come together to explore the creative process and, despite their differences, experience a journey wherein they can create something new together.

Chuck views creativity as a language that can be used to overcome situations where words are difficult.

PHOTOGRAPHED 3/1/2010

Kathy Kelly

I have a strong belief that we should experiment with nonviolence as a means to change our world, that nonviolence can change our world from being a place where people are always vulnerable to wars being waged against civilian populations . . . that if we stop and slow down and think about it and really practice nonviolence, we could change that. That's what I want my life to be about. It's a fiercely urgent time to practice nonviolence, so this is a part of that. I'm a war tax refuser. I won't pay for weapons and I haven't, since 1980, paid any kind of federal income tax. I'm also someone who has been part of peace teams in various war zones: in Sarajevo, in Nicaragua prior to that, in Iraq during the first Gulf War, in Iraq in 2003 during the shock and awe invasion. I was in Lebanon in the 2006 Israeli war against Lebanon. I was in Gaza in 2009, and I just came back from Pakistan.

Kathy Kelly is a peace activist and co-coordinator for Voices for Creative Nonviolence. She has visited war zones around the world in an effort to experience war firsthand.

Kathy has not paid federal taxes since 1980 because of her conviction that doing so would make her complicit in war.

She believes that we all need to slow down in order to explore the global ramifications of our decisions and our lifestyles.

When I list all of those war zones, I think I must sound like I'm a little crazy, but I think that we have to keep experimenting with the further invention of nonviolence. And when one experiences war from the perspective of the people who are more or less in front of the gun as targets or under the drone, if you will . . . standing or sitting or sleeping with a family that is trapped, that can't go anywhere, you understand a very different perspective about war.

82

Daniel Chacón

In recent years, it seems the voices of the people have been kind of pushed aside. We're expecting politicians to solve our problems and I think that's wrong. I think it's time that we get to hear what people think peace is and what can be done to achieve peace all over the world.

To live a peaceful life . . . if you're going to promote any change, I think you should start first within you, and then spread it out into your environment. A lot of people say peace is a state of mind. Ninety percent is how you react to things. Ten percent is actually what happens to you. It's an interesting concept . . . I've tried it and it works for me. How you react to things has an impact on peace. Because a lot of the times, if you find conflicts between people, you rewind the tape and you find it was a really insignificant thing. How you react to that insignificant thing can have a big impact as to the outcome between two people or the outcome between two nations.

You should not ever forget about the little things, because the little things are the ones that happen almost every day and how you deal with them is the key.

Daniel Chacón was born in El Salvador and moved to the United States when he was 13 years old. Today he is part owner of Arte Hispano, a store that sells arts and crafts from Latin America. He is studying business management and philosophy at Hamline University.

Daniel believes that we need to assess our own views constantly and consider the possibility that we may not have all of the answers. He says that even though he may not always understand someone, he will always try to be understanding.

84

Harry Williams Jr.

I'm 61 years old. How I define peace is a function of where I am in chronological age and probably historical age, too. At this juncture, I'm seeking and striving after personal peace. I want to make peace with my great anger at America. I want to make peace with myself. I want to make peace with the people I hold dear and close — my bosom-buddy friends, my thick-and-thin friends. I'm defining peace as a more humane and positive orientation toward self and others. But I don't think I will ever become peaceful if that means accepting the horrific things that have happened to people of African descent in the United States. I don't ever want to make peace with that.

I see the world as it is, and I believe evil marches in the world. I believe that people do evil for any number of reasons. I don't like it, but I accept that. And as it pertains to the historical experiences of black people in the United States, my reading of history, and my living for 61 years, I can no longer afford to be an internal, unabashed, unaltered optimist. I must make peace unwillingly with reality.

There is a great richness and a great complexity to life. I tell my students, "Life is dirty. Life is messy." The birth process is messy, and I saw my mother dying of cancer. I wasn't there at the moment she died, but I know that she suffered. I have to come to terms with that, and that's all part of the peace process. Shall I dare use that term in this sense? That richness, that complexity, that complicatedness is what gives us our humanity. I may fault Americans for being too optimistic, but then you may come back to me and say, "What are the benefits of pessimism?"

Striving after peace is complicated, dirty, but ultimately rewarding — and perhaps elusive.

86

Harry Williams Jr. is a professor of history. Among the courses he teaches are "African American History," "Black Atlantic History," which focuses on the relationship between Ghana and the United States, and "U.S. History from 1865 to 1945."

Harry views the world from what he calls "a tragic conception of history and a tragic conception of life," which means that "we accept the bitter and the sweet."

Lynne Zotalis

You don't know what tomorrow's going to be. You don't know if that's the last time you'll see that person. I've had such a tumultuous relationship with my parents and my sister and my brother. There have been long periods of time where we have not communicated at all. But I ultimately have to come back to this question: Is that how you want it to end if that's the last time you're going to see them, if that's the last time you're ever going to talk to them? I know it's kind of a fatalistic way to think about relationships, but I've had that experience. My husband and I were madly in love for 31 years. We had a wonderful relationship. And I took a scrapbook that I had compiled secretly to Mexico with us, and I gave it to him. And we had our anniversary. It was a Tuesday. And he read it and it was everything I wanted to say to him about our life, our marriage, our children, what he meant to me — and the next day, he died. He cried when he read it. He was so just moved and so tender, and I think, "Wow, how lucky is that?" I got to say those things to him — although he knew I felt that way all of our life. To put those things on paper — it's a treasure.

Lynne Zotalis is a writer who participates in a peace and social justice group called "Writing Peace into the World." She believes that peace within our own small sphere of influence is needed before we can ever hope for peace in the larger world.

Lynne talks about losing her husband suddenly, and how fortunate she feels that she had given him an anniversary gift the night before he died — a scrapbook she had made for him that said how much she loved him and how much their relationship meant to her.

Working through that loss led her to re-examine a long-held interest in writing, which is one of the ways she experiences peace in her life.

88

Scott Augustine

At its heart, the Peace House Africa project — taking care of orphans — is about peace. It's my belief that it is very difficult to have peace in the world if there is a lack of hope. People must have hope. Hope for a brighter future for themselves . . . hope for a brighter future for their families. When you have hope, you are busy doing positive things, you don't have time or interest in doing negative things. It's when you feel hopeless that suddenly the negative things in life become much more interesting to you.

Scott Augustine is CEO of a medical device company. A decade ago, he established a project in Tanzania called Peace House Africa, which works to educate AIDS orphans in the country where he spent several years of his childhood while his father worked as a missionary.

Scott views education as the best chance for hope, and he believes that when people are hopeful about their future, that can lead to peace.

What I'd like to focus on is something that can be changed . . . and that is, you can educate. Education not only gives hope to people — and I believe that vastly increases the chances of maintaining peace — but also education can kind of moderate the effects of tribalism and the effects of religion that frequently lead the other direction. Of the treatable causes, you might say, I believe education goes farther toward giving hope for the future than really anything else you can do.

90

Najm Abed Askori

When God created people, he created them in different tribes, different nations. The purpose of that? They got to know each other, they got to understand each other. This can be fulfilled only by a peaceful life. Peace is much cheaper than war, and it is the most effective way for people.

When we have a peaceful life in Iraq, certainly we will buy the best of the goods and the products. And we are very sure American goods, American cars, American agriculture are the best in the world. So we will be probably the first customers in that region to [buy] the U.S. products. We need it because it is the best, and probably the companies here need [us].

Peace is to live in harmony with all people around. Peace is a name of God also. Do you know that in the Holy Qur'an, God has 99 names? One of them is *Peace.* Es Salam. Es Salam is a name of God. That is why we very much like to see peaceful lives, and peace dominating the globe. I personally do not like to see any conflicts in any area. This can be achieved by the right politics, right policies, done by first the superpower, and then by the neighboring countries. Everything could be solved by dialog. We are differentiated from other creatures, we have a tongue. We have vocabulary, and we can use words, whatever it is . . . hard, strong, stiff, but only by tongue, not by hands, not by arms.

America is a very powerful country. It should maintain good relations with other nations, especially their allies. And Iraq is one of their allies.

Najm Abed Askori is an assistant professor of physics at the University of Kufa in Iraq. He participates in research to document the effects of depleted uranium munitions used by U.S. forces in Iraq. Designed to penetrate hardened targets, depleted uranium remains toxic for generations, affecting military and civilian populations alike.

Najm is a member of the Muslim Peacemaker Teams in Iraq. In October 2009 he traveled to Minnesota as part of a delegation of Iraqis who are establishing a sister city program between Minneapolis and Najaf, Iraq.

92

Rabbi Marcia Zimmerman

For me, being in relationships is the ultimate requirement of peace. You can't bring two people, two nations, two worlds into a peaceful connection without a relationship.

In my own experience in interfaith dialogues, we can all live on this ideal plain — peace and understanding. And we can all kind of agree on so much, and then we get down to the details and it can fall apart. So relationships go back and forth and up and down and things are complicated.

But we've made a commitment not to back away from the table. And when one of us is feeling a bit vulnerable, the others remind that person that we're not backing away from the table, that we value each other, and so it is an interesting process and it's unfolded in many different ways.

94

Rabbi Marcia Zimmerman is senior rabbi at Temple Israel in Minneapolis. She participates in regular interfaith dialogue with clergy from other religions, and recognizes the benefits and challenges of working with such groups.

Marcia draws on a Talmudic text that speaks of several layers of peace, and she explains that peace is not a linear process — it is an ever-evolving process — and we may find that we make progress one day only to lose it the next.

We have to get down to what's real. Not the ideal, not the hopes, not the political view, not the value that's coming from a particular community that might be somewhat offensive to another community. We need to come together and we need to understand what is real and true and then we can begin to talk.

You have to bring things pretty much down to their fundamental level in order to speak to one another, in order to create peace. And you don't even know the assumptions you bring. That's why I love being at the table of interfaith dialogue. I am always confronted with my assumptions and I am there to confront others about their assumptions. For me, that's holy work. That's absolutely holy work, holy conversation.

Jeff Kennedy

You talk about peace . . . I've watched men in jail who have no common background . . . they used to hand cigarettes out in the jail . . . and they would give each other a cigarette . . . when one was in need, another one gave. The other one not worried about who came from where. I've watched the alcoholics and the drunks on the street . . . one has 17 cents, the other has 65 cents. And they all come together on that common ground, at that common moment, and they go buy themselves a bottle with no argument, or worry about their ethnic backgrounds or whatever.

I'm 52 years old now and it took probably 50 years for me to really come to peace, and come to terms fully with what peace meant to me. I went back to Detroit to visit, and in recent years I experienced in America the first time, a full family intact, having dinner. And it brought me to tears because my whole life, I had never seen an American black family . . . eat dinner at the dinner table all together.

So when I think of world peace, I just think of us all having a meal together, sitting down, everyone from every tongue and place on the planet. We have all different walks, all different religions, but we come together for meditation, not worrying about each other's address, zip code, phone number, whether they're homeless, or whether they have a job or a great job. Those diplomas and certificates and all of those accomplishments mean nothing until we can just check our pride pistols at the door and come in all humility together and just walk together. That's what peace is to me.

Jeff Kennedy has spent time on the streets in rough neighborhoods and time behind bars, yet he has found a peace that has helped him weather life's storms.

Jeff believes that often we wait for life's tragedies before we reach out to one another, but he sees hope in the small, kind gestures that even total strangers can show one another in every day situations.

PHOTOGRAPHED 5/14/2009

97

Marion Vance

How do you try to measure the intangible elements? The tendency is to try to put a number on everything, and to think something is real if you can count it or measure it. Many of [life's] benefits, you can't put on a scale and see how much they weigh. Things like self-esteem and cooperation and strengthening of organizations so that even the poor people have a voice in how things operate. How do you put a number on that? How do you measure it?

At the moment, our measure of success is pretty unilateral. It's the almighty dollar, or the equivalent of it. As long as the only measure of success is money and how much of it you make, then anything goes. The end justifies the means and as long as you're rich, it doesn't matter how many bloody bodies you trampled to get there.

Marion Vance is the retired director of learning and evaluation for Inter-American Foundation, an NGO that supported development work in Latin America. The organization tried to help some of the poorest people in the hemisphere feel like they had a stronger voice in their own affairs.

Marion is interested in exploring how we measure the intangible things in our lives that add so much value. And in the pursuit of a more peaceful world, she believes it is important for us to create a new measuring stick for success.

As long as your value or self-worth is measured by how much money you make, by how big your house is, by how many boats you can buy, I don't think there's much hope. If those things suddenly become not goals to be worked toward, but things that people are a little repulsed by, oh boy! You know, why does so and so really need eight houses and 14 boats and $600 million a year?

Instead of seeing [materialism] as the pinnacle of success, if that begins to be seen as self-serving, then maybe people will start to strive for something else. If we measured worth by, "What did you do today to begin to crack the problem of homelessness," or "What did you do today to make sure that all children get an even start when they go into school?"

We have to change how we define success. It's a question of definitions to me.

PHOTOGRAPHED 2/24/2010

Julius C. Collins III

I think that there's nothing wrong with being Afrocentric or, you know, having an affinity for Italians if you're Italian, or to be proud of being Irish if you're Irish. I think this is what makes us beautiful. This is actually what makes us strong and smart and this is what's going to make us last. But when you plant a whole row of elm trees, they get Dutch elm disease. You have to mix in. You have to cross-pollinate. That's the essence of survival for me, and my lack of peace comes when people don't acknowledge that my happiness and my survival is directly connected to yours.

Julius C. Collins III is a singer and a songwriter. He strives to set a tone in his music and in his life that will allow a space for peace.

Julius grew up in the foster care system and learned to keep his guard up as a defense mechanism. Years later he learned he was happier when he let his guard down.

He is married to a woman who went to law school, but who now works as a gardener — a process that convinced Julius of the importance of being true to who you are and what you want to do in life.

I think it's so great that I can be married to a woman who's Caucasian and not have to worry about crosses being burned on my lawn. I know about these things. I have had conversations with grandparents and great uncles and, you know, some of that stuff is really terrifying. There's none of that for us. I don't get called names as I go down the street, not usually. So I think we've come a long ways, but my anger is when we can't come that rest of the way. It's like, c'mon, y'all, just think what diseases could be solved, what could be created as a result of us just letting down our guard and seeing each other and having faith that there's something beyond the stereotype.

100

Lisa Albrecht

For me peace is about justice. Believe in peace, work for justice — there are bumper stickers that say that. And justice for me is the notion of what's called distributive justice, meaning nobody gets seconds until everyone gets firsts. Until there's distributive justice there can't really be peace, so my first inclination is not to talk about peace as the world without war, because I think if we had justice there wouldn't be war and there wouldn't be the kinds of conflicts we have now.

I think we have what I call pockets of hope. We have lots of pockets where there's incredible work going on for peace and for justice, but the pockets don't connect to make the bigger movement. We have a critical mass of people who want to make the world more peaceful and just, but we haven't figured out how to work together.

If we were to build social movements that were genuinely and authentically about working together . . . and if enough of us could stand in solidarity and do whatever has to be done to work for justice and for peace, maybe we could change the world. The history of the United States has been a history of social movements changing things. The civil rights movement, the women's movement, the GLBT movement. Policy changes. People with power have to listen when you have a critical mass of people.

Lisa Albrecht is a professor at the University of Minnesota, where she oversees an undergraduate minor in social justice.

Lisa sees the need to pursue peace and justice with "beloved community," a term used by Martin Luther King Jr. that encompasses not only one's blood family, but also a circle of loved ones who care for one another and hold one another accountable.

She believes that change builds from the bottom up, and she is encouraged by the way today's social activists are engaging the community through social media and other tools that were not available to us a generation ago.

102

Roy Martin

I revel in bonding with people who are completely different from me. I've made strong relationships wherever I've gone, and I'm passionate about getting to understand people.

I've always wanted to do something internationally. I am idealistic and I like to work hard. I've never felt better than when I was living in the homes of rural Peruvian families. We come from such different worlds, but we were on the same wavelength. Mixing mud with mothers and smiling and making faces at kids. Trying to learn their indigenous language. Teaching them English, which was a futile effort, but fun nonetheless. We laughed and joked. It sounds cheesy, but every day was inspiring. I was doing work with a purpose that I was passionate about. And that's how I want to live every day of my life.

Peace to me lies in people's ability to connect with one other — the power of caring and how that is manifested. It doesn't happen on a political or a spiritual level for me; it's on a human-to-human level. It comes from a touch or showing someone compassion and genuine love — these are deep and valuable human capabilities.

Peace is a compassionate interaction with anybody at any level. Opening up your mind and being willing to look deeper and see a side of someone that you wouldn't have seen otherwise is such an easy thing to do, but it's also a really hard thing to do. It's the only right thing to do, and I think the only way to live a happy life is by doing the right thing.

104

Roy Martin is a history major from Brooklyn, New York, who recently spent a summer in Peru on a project designed to slow deforestation by installing fuel-efficient wood stoves in village homes. The project sought to curb wood consumption while simultaneously reducing illnesses related to smoke inhalation.

Roy found his greatest reward through connecting on a human level with people from very different backgrounds.

PHOTOGRAPHED 2/15/2010

Marie Braun

I believe in a concept called formation through action. Any action we take affects who we are. I am one of those people who are out on the street. I believe we need this public witness. And also we need people doing actions that may be outside their comfort level. It's going to have a great impact on their life. It's also for us. We do this partially for ourselves.

There's a story about a man who was sitting out by a nuclear site in one of the Dakotas. And someone said, "Why do you keep sitting here? Nobody sees you. You're not getting any media. Why do you keep doing this? You're not influencing anyone." And he said, "I'm doing it for myself. So that the powers that be don't change me."

Marie Braun is a retired therapist and a committed peace activist. She organizes weekly vigils and believes it is important to have a constant, visible opposition to war. Marie says that showing her opposition publicly not only presents the opportunity to change others, but also presents the chance to change herself.

She believes that our elected officials do not always look out for the good of the citizens, but instead often serve the interests of the corporations who donate to their election funds.

I always have hope. That's what keeps me going. Staying involved gives me hope and I think that's why I work hard in the peace movement. We see that people change. People get involved and our actions do affect other people. I see it rippling out, and we don't know what happens as a result of what we're doing. I think often that we tend to focus on ourselves and say, "You must have peace within yourself before you can look at these bigger issues and work on these bigger issues." For me there's a better way. I need to work on both myself and the broader issues and actually it's my involvement in the broader issues and my training in nonviolence that have helped me to become a more peaceful person rather than the other way around.

106

Zafar Siddiqui

Actually, I get my understanding of peace by the religion that I follow. Because . . . the word Islam comes from the root word in Arabic called *salam,* meaning peace . . . so it becomes imperative that I understand peace in a much deeper way.

I think that if anybody reads the Qur'an in its entirety . . . without any ulterior motive, then the message that it gives is nothing but peace. But if someone wants to achieve their political goals, they can always use the cut and paste approach. You take out a verse and use it out of context for your own goal. I think it happens in other religious traditions, too. [If] people focus on only one aspect, ignoring the bigger context, you are able to prove anything, from any book.

I would say that the more Muslims know about Islam, the more centrist they become. One of the biggest problems I see in the Muslim world is that they have gone away from Islam. As a result, we are seeing all of these problems where there is so much injustice, violence, and other things. But it's my belief that if a Muslim follows Islam fully — how it is supposed to be practiced — then he or she will be a great moderate person in the sense of getting along with each other, because the Islamic teachings talk about how you have to get along with people of other faiths. In fact, Islam actually says, call Jews, Christians, and Muslims to common terms, to the fact that we all worship one God, the God of Abraham.

Zafar Siddiqui is an American Muslim who was born in India. He serves on the board of directors for Al-Amal School, the first all-Islamic K–12 school in Minnesota, and he leads the Islamic Resource Group, which is dedicated to educating people about Islam and Muslims.

Zafar defends the peaceful nature of Islam as a religion, and points out that fringe elements have misused the religion for their own purposes, just as radicals from other religions have done throughout history.

108

selected discussion topics

This book explores the meaning of peace, but I will be the first to tell you that it does not contain all of the answers. My greatest hope for this project is that it will help encourage others to engage in conversations about peace and explore how they might contribute to making the world a more peaceful place through building understanding among people and recognizing the common humanity that connects us all.

Below is a list of questions that can be used to explore the subject further, either on your own, or with others. Many of the questions are the same ones that I used in my interviews with subjects for this project. Others are prompts that I use in the writing workshops for *a peace of my mind.*

I encourage you to spend time with these questions and engage others in them. Only by making peace a part of our public dialogue can we hope to make progress toward a more peaceful world.

DISCUSSION TOPICS:

1 What does peace mean to you?

2 How do you work toward peace in your life?

3 What are some of the obstacles you encounter in your pursuit of peace?

4 What is required for a peaceful life? A peaceful home? A peaceful world?

5 Talk about the relationship between inner peace and outer peace.

6 Explore where your personal understanding of peace comes from.

7 Recall a time when you saw a great example of peace.

8 Recall a time when you failed in achieving a peaceful resolution. What went wrong?

9 Which subject in *a peace of my mind* resonates with you? Why?

10 Which subject in *a peace of my mind* surprised or challenged you? Why?

11 What are some ways that you can build a more peaceful relationship with someone who has a very different viewpoint from your own?

12 Talk about an adversary and find some good in that person. How is that helpful?

13 What can you do in your own life that can make the world a more peaceful place?

14 When do you find your notions of peace most challenged? Why?

15 What can we do to build more capacity for peace in our world? Is there a way that a culture of peace can be taught or passed on to future generations?

index

III

Odeh Muhawesh
Page 17

Marge Sullivan
Page 19

Gopal Khanna
Page 21

Jennifer McNally
Page 23

Melvin Carter Jr.
Page 25

Jeff Blodgett
Page 27

Morgan Murphy
Page 29

Luyen Phan
Page 31

Mark Williams
Page 33

Hudlin Wagner
Page 35

Eric Gibson
Page 37

Rabbi Amy Eilberg
Page 39

Jamal Hashi
Page 41

Al Quie
Page 43

The McDonald Sisters, left to right; Jane, Brigid, Kate, and Rita
Page 45

Richard Rittmaster
Page 47

Flora Tsukayama
Page 49

Michael Kiesow Moore
Page 51

Catherine Mamer
Page 53

V. David Schwantes
Page 55

Imani Jaafar-Mohammad
Page 57

Mel Duncan
Page 59

Rev. Andre Golike
Page 61

Barbara Nordstrom-Loeb
Page 63

Jack Nelson-Pallmeyer
Page 65

Khant Khant Kyaw
Page 67

Rev. Harry Wendt
Page 69

Kelly Connole
Page 71

Sami Rasouli
Page 73

Marlene Jezierski
Page 75

David Harris
Page 77

Kim Smith
Page 79

Chuck Hoffman
Page 81

Kathy Kelly
Page 83

Daniel Chacón
Page 85

Harry Williams Jr.
Page 87

Lynne Zotalis
Page 89

Scott Augustine
Page 91

Najm Abed Askori
Page 93

Rabbi Marcia Zimmerman
Page 95

Jeff Kennedy
Page 97

Marion Vance
Page 99

Julius C. Collins III
Page 101

Lisa Albrecht
Page 103

Roy Martin
Page 105

Marie Braun
Page 107

Zafar Siddiqui
Page 109

selected resources

In the process of working on *a peace of my mind*, I have come across amazing people and organizations working for peace. Their work takes many forms including activism, education, social services, and inspiration, yet all of it leads us in the right direction — toward relationships, understanding, and peace.

Some of the websites listed below are directly related to the subjects who were interviewed for *a peace of my mind*, and others are organizations I have learned about while working on the project. The list is by no means exhaustive, but it is a place to begin. I encourage you to look into some of these organizations and see if there is a way for you to help or become involved. Or find another group whose mission matches your passions. There is work to be done. If we each do a little, together we can accomplish a lot.

A Peace of My Mind
Exploring the meaning of peace one story at a time
www.apeaceofmymind.net

Beyond the Mirror
Working for peace in homes by distributing information about unhealthy/violent relationships, suggesting ways to help individuals in such relationships, and empowering and affirming victim/survivors
www.beyond-the-mirror.org

Crossways International
Sharing God's timeless story worldwide
www.crossways.org

Empty Bowls
An international grassroots effort to fight hunger
www.emptybowls.net

Heatherlyn Music
Considering how we each are conduits of peace and hope in our world
www.heatherlynmusic.com

Genesis + Art
Creating pathways to God through scripture and art, nourishing the creative spirit
www.genesisartstudio.com

Inter-American Foundation
Dedicated to improving the well-being and civic engagement of the organized poor in Latin America and the Caribbean
www.iaf.gov

Iraqi & American Reconciliation Project
Connecting Iraqis and Americans in art, education, and cultural exchange programs in order to build peace
www.reconciliationproject.org

Islamic Resource Group
Building bridges of understanding through education
www.irgmn.org

Lutheran Partners in Global Ministry
Face to face and hand in hand — meeting needs around the world
www.lutheranpartners.org

Minnesota Alliance of Peacemakers
Creating a culture of peace and nonviolence
www.mapm.org

**Muslim-Christian Dialogue Center
University of St. Thomas**
Fostering mutual understanding and cooperation among Muslims and Christians through academic and community dialogue grounded in the Qur'anic and Christian traditions
www.stthomas.edu/mcdc

Muslim Peacemaker Teams
Working for peace and human rights in Iraq
www.mpt-iraq.org

Nonviolent Peaceforce
Fostering dialogue among parties in conflict and
providing a protective presence for threatened civilians
www.nonviolentpeaceforce.org

Peace Corps
Serving in the cause of peace by living and working
in developing countries
http://www.peacecorps.gov

Peace House Africa
Educating AIDS orphans. Creating brighter futures
www.peacehouseafrica.org

Peace House Community
A gathering place for homeless people and others
in an urban neighborhood
www.peacehousecommunity.org

Peace and Justice Studies Association
Creating a just and peaceful world through research,
education, and action
www.peacejusticestudies.org

Peace and Social Justice Writers Group
Consciously exploring the nature of peace in order to
renew and maintain a sense of hope for the future
www.michaelkiesowmoore.com/PeaceWriters.html

Project on Civic Reflection
Helping civic groups build capacity, commitment,
and community through reading and discussion
www.civicreflection.org

Shambhala Buddhism
Based in the belief that every human being
has a fundamental nature of goodness, warmth,
and intelligence
www.shambhala.org

Shinnyo-en Foundation
Helping to build more caring communities by
supporting educational programs that engage and
inspire young people in meaningful acts of service
www.sef.org

Sisters of St. Joseph of Carondelet
Committed to continuing Jesus's mission in the world
by responding to the needs of our time
www.csjstpaul.org

United for Peace & Justice
From the local to the global, connecting movements
for justice and peace
www.unitedforpeace.org

Veterans for Peace
An educational and humanitarian organization
dedicated to the abolishment of war
www.veteransforpeace.org

Voices for Creative Nonviolence
Committed to active nonviolent resistance
to U.S. war-making
www.vcnv.org

Wellstone Action!
A national center for training and leadership
development in the progressive movement
www.wellstone.org

Wisdom Ways
Exploring the crossways of Christian spirituality,
womanist and feminist thought, ecumenical and
inter-religious conversations, and social action for
justice and peace
www.wisdomwayscenter.org

Women Against Military Madness
Creating a system of social equality, self-determination,
and justice through education, action, and the
empowerment of women
www.worldwidewamm.org

about this book

I am grateful to the many people who made this book possible, especially each of the subjects who took the time to share their thoughts and wisdom included in these pages. Each of them, in their own way, is doing great work to make our world a better place, and I am honored and humbled to have gotten to know them.

I consider myself blessed by the friends and family who patiently encouraged me through this entire process, serving as sounding board and rudder as I explored how to bring this project from concept to reality. A special thank you is owed to my wife, Karen, for her patience and unending support as I pursue my many projects, and to my good friends Sandra Anderson, Wade Barry, and Evan Hansen for their many insights along this road.

Several long-time colleagues have offered up their expertise to make this project come to life. Jonathan Hankin's design produced this series as a beautiful traveling exhibit in 2010 with funding from the Minnesota State Arts Board. The exhibit now travels to venues nationwide. Teresa Scalzo is a brilliant editor whose careful editing has saved me from many embarrassing errors and omissions. And Barbara Koster has designed the pages of this book with the sweet sensibility that only she can bring to a project.

Finally, I want to thank each of the 92 backers in our Kickstarter campaign who made the printing of this book possible. I am grateful for each pledge. Large or small, each one was a vote of support and a voice of encouragement as we built a community of individuals who were interested in sharing this message of peace with a larger audience. The names listed at right deserve special thanks for having contributed substantially to the effort of bringing this book into the world.

With peace and gratitude,

JOHN NOLTNER

Sandra Anderson

Wade Barry

Break Bread Hospitality

Edward & Shirley Buxton

Kathy & Dan Daggett

Sue Eleuterio

The Ken & Gail Ericson
Family

Rick & Linda Glasgow

Mark & Carla Hillman

Randy & Melissa Hoepner

Richard Y. Kain

Jason Krumm

Ken & Margie Little

Karen & Phil Luck

Catherine Murray Mamer

Donna & Michael Meyer

Rick & Bonnie Mickelson

Jeff Noltner

Don Noltner

Gordon & Betty Olson

Thomas & Maren Ortmeier

The George & Nancy Schaaf
Family

Robert & Kathy Simmons

Doris Thimmesh

David & Denise Thoen

Jim & Lori Thomson

Lori Anne Yang

Barry Yeoman

Jon & Anita Young

Thomas & Meredith Young

www.apeaceofmymind.net

ISBN: 978-0-615-53068-0

Designed by Barbara Koster
Typefaces are Mrs. Eaves and
Vista from Emigre

Printed on recycled paper